LETTER TO MARCELLINUS ON THE PSALMS

SPIRITUAL WISDOM FOR TODAY

ATHANASIUS OF ALEXANDRIA

Translated by
JOEL C. ELOWSKY

Copyright © 2021 by ICCS Press, Inc.

2nd printing, 2023.

All rights reserved. No part of this publication may be reproduced, stored in a retrieval system, or transmitted in any form or by any means — electronic, mechanical, photocopy, recording, or any other — except for brief quotations in printed reviews, without the prior permission of the publisher.

Requests for information should be addressed to: ICCS Press, 616 Prospect St, New Haven, CT 06511

ISBN 978-1-62428-013-9

Cover design: *speersdesign.com*

Cover Image: Michael Glerup

1

INTRODUCTION TO ATHANASIUS' LETTER TO MARCELLINUS

Athanasius of Alexandria (ca. 298-373) was first and foremost a pastor at heart. He was bishop of the church in Alexandria off and on again from 328 until the time of his death 45 years later. He grew up during a time of intense persecution initiated under Diocletian (303-311). The persecution lasted from his childhood through his early teenage years. His parents were wealthy enough to secure a good secular education for him, but his formation as a churchman and theologian no doubt occurred during his time with Bishop Alexander of Alexandria (312-328) where he spent most of his formative years as a teenager and young adult. He became Alexander's secretary as well as a deacon in the church under Alexander's tutelage. During that time, two issues that came to the fore were the Miletian Schism and the Arian controversy. Both of these issues would come to a head at the Council of Nicaea (325) which the deacon Athanasius attended along with his bishop. The Arian controversy, especially, would dominate much of his writing after he succeeded Alexander as bishop in 328. His opposition to Arianism in its various forms, and the inevitable politics which accompanied it, would be the primary cause for the five different exiles he experienced during his time as Patriarch. One can gauge the ebb and flow of the Arian controversy simply by looking at the timing of his exiles. But the subject of the *Letter to Marcellinus* deals only tangentially with the Arians.

The *Letter to Marcellinus* was written in response to a letter he received from a sick friend named Marcellinus. It was most likely written in the latter part of Athanasius' career, perhaps sometime during the early 360s, according to Craig Blaising.[1] The identity of the Marcellinus to whom the letter is addressed is nowhere stated in the letter. All we are told is that he has been afflicted with an ongoing illness which has incapacitated him for a time, allowing him to focus on the study of Scripture and, more specifically, the Psalms. Athanasius does remark in the opening paragraph that he is pleased that Marcellinus has not neglected the "ascesis" which could perhaps indicate that Marcellinus was some type of clergy, although there were perhaps laity who also engaged in such a practice. The evidence in the letter itself, however, would seem to lean towards someone who was clergy. In chapter 3.50 of his *Defense Against the Arians* there is a Marcellinus listed in the first paragraph of that section among those bishops who subscribed to the Council of Sardica (344). Later, in the same document, there is another Marcellinus listed among the deacons of the church at Alexandria, included in a letter to the bishops of Tyre who were accusing Athanasius of clergy misconduct. In some documents it appears as though Marcellinus' name was confused with Marcellus of Ancyra,[2] so this could be a possibility, albeit a rather slim one. Athanasius also mentions a government official named Marcellinus, referring to the "Consulate of Marcellinus" in his *De Synodis* 25 and again in his *Festal Letter* 13 (341 AD). But it is doubtful that such a government official would have been practicing the ascetical discipline which Athanasius references in his opening remarks—although we need not rule out the possibility out of hand. The most logical referent, however, would seem to be either the Alexandrian deacon Marcellinus, or perhaps the bishop Marcellinus who subscribed to the Council of Sardica, or some other Marcellinus of which we are unaware, since Marcellinus was a common name at the time.

Ultimately, the identity of the recipient is not as important as the occasion for the letter. Marcellinus is looking for spiritual guidance on how to read the Psalms and he appeals to the Patriarch of Alexandria for advice. The Psalms were the prayer book of the ancient church. Prior to Athanasius, Origen of Alexandria had begun his exegetical endeavors by first writing a commentary on Psalm 15. He later commented on many other Psalms, perhaps even attempting a second commentary with his discovery of the *Quinta* and *Sexta* versions of the Septuagint which he included in his *Hexapla*. In Athanasius' own day, the famed bishop and historian, Eusebius of Caesarea, wrote a commentary on the entire Psalter, perhaps utilizing some of Origen's work he had in his library there at Caesarea. The Psalms were perhaps one of the most widely commented on books of the Bible during the period of the early church fathers right up until the time of Luther and the Reformation. Luther devoted his own first exegetical study to the Psalms.

The Psalms were the prayer book of the early church. They were used daily in the liturgy, but also in the devotional lives of the faithful who memorized large portions of the Psalter—if not the Psalter in its entirety. Athanasius understood with St. Paul that even Christians often do not know what to pray for, or how to offer up prayer, but that the Spirit is there to help us in our weakness[3] and has even provided the words for our prayers in the Psalms.[4] The Psalms also are a wonderful diagnostic and pedagogical tool, Athanasius says, teaching us to recognize the inner movements in our own souls as though we were looking in a mirror as we sing them.[5] But they not only teach us to diagnose and recognize what is going on in the innermost part of our being. They also provide what we need to say or do in order to bring healing to our souls.[6] Athanasius believed that the Psalms, more than any other book of Scripture, were written to speak directly to the soul. They anticipated every condition of life that human beings undergo—and not only anticipated them, but provided the proper prescription for what ails the human condition.

There are two reasons why the Psalms speak so directly to the soul: (1) the Psalms were written in such a way that the words actually become the property of the one speaking them at that moment. David may have written the words, but they become the words of whoever is chanting or singing them at the moment.[7] This does not happen in quite the same as with other portions of Scripture, Athanasius points out, such as with the historical narratives or the words of Old Testament figures such as Moses or Elijah. No one would dare claim the words of Moses or Elijah as their own, or deign to speak them as if they were anyone else's but Moses' or Elijah's. But the Psalms are different. By design of the Spirit, they are written in such a way that whoever speaks them, sings them, shouts them—does so as if they were their own.[8] (2) A second characteristic of the Psalms that conforms them to the contours of the soul is the fact that they were meant to be sung. The more simple-minded, Athanasius says, think the primary reason the Psalms are to be sung is because the music is pleasing to the ear and so we sing the Psalms for enjoyment.[9] While this may be true, he thinks such reasoning too facile and so he points to two reasons that the Psalms are to be sung: First, music provides for a freer, less restricted expression of words, especially when they need to be employed in praise to God. Secondly, the Psalms speak to the whole range of human emotions and inner movements of the soul—from anger, to desire, to the contemplation of reason. But the Psalms bring these wide ranging movements of the soul into harmony with the mind and the body so that the person does not find himself "discordant or at variance with himself."[10] He employs the analogy of a symphony: many different instruments across the spectrum of sound play in harmony together to produce a single symphony of sound. If one uses the Psalms in this way, he is using them properly because they will speak to the different temperaments of his soul.

Athanasius tells us in the beginning of the letter that he learned how to read the Psalms from an old man who explained them to him with "a certain grace and persuasiveness" that he thought worthwhile to pass on.[11] The bulk of his letter to Marcellinus then rehearses what he learned from the old man as to which Psalms speak to the various situations of life. In effect, the letter serves as an introductory guide for using the Psalms in pastoral and personal care. After some initial discussion about how the Psalms are similar and yet unique to other portions of Scripture, as we rehearsed above, he delves into categorizing the Psalms according to those "that speak in narrative form, in exhortations, in prophecies, in the form of prayer, as well as in confession."[12] He then spends many chapters traversing through the entirety of the Psalter—or at least most of it—indicating more specifically how each Psalm speaks to the various conditions of people. Athanasius often uses variations on the following format: If you _____, recite or sing Psalm _____. For example, "If you are suffering persecution from your own people, and you have many assembled against you, recite the third Psalm. If in such affliction you called to the Lord and you want to give thanks that he heard you, sing Psalms 4, 75 and 116."[13] In this way, one can know where to turn in the Psalms to receive help in time of need.

Athanasius believed that the Psalms were divinely inspired, which is why they are so helpful to the human soul. He describes the Psalter as a choice garden filled with a variety of fruit for the soul—all of which feed the human condition. "For whether there is a need for repentance or confession, or tribulation and trials overtake someone, or someone is persecuted, or delivered from those who were plotting against him, or if someone is deeply grieved and troubled and suffers in some way ... or he sees himself prospering while his enemy is hindered, or he wants to sing or to give thanks or to bless the Lord—he can find instructions in the divine Psalms."[14] The Psalms can even benefit those engaged in spiritual warfare as we see in both the Old and New Testaments.[15] But such warfare requires practice and intimate knowledge of the Psalms so that, led by the Spirit, you can choose wisely which Psalms speak to the condition you are in.

There are a couple of final notes of explanation needed for this introduction. The translation is based on the Greek text found in Migne's *Patrologia Graeca,* vol. 27. Further information about the transmission of the text can be found there. Migne's text would seem to be the most reliable edition we have at the moment. In addition, the reader should know that Athanasius read the Old Testament in the Greek translation of his day, known as the Septuagint (LXX). The wording of the text may sometimes differ from what readers are used to. This is also true of some of his New Testament quotations. In addition, the numbering of the Psalms in the Septuagint is different than what readers will find in their Hebrew or English Bibles. In order to make it easier to look up the Psalms Athanasius is referencing, we have converted all of the Septuagint numbering to the corresponding English and Hebrew numbering. Every now and then brackets are included in the text where the Hebrew combines two Greek Psalms or the Greek combines two Hebrew Psalms. As a point of reference, I have included a handy guide for comparing the Septuagint and Hebrew numbering of the Psalms:

Hebrew Psalms	Greek Psalms
1-8	1-8
9-10	9
11-113	10-112
114-115	113
116	114-115
117-146	116-145
147	146-147
148-150	148-150
Not Present	151

Joel C. Elowsky, Translator and Editor
Feast of the Resurrection, 2016

2

ATHANASIUS: LETTER TO MARCELLINUS

I am amazed at your resolve in Christ, beloved Marcellinus. For both in terms of your present trial, and indeed the many things you have endured in it, you have borne them well—and without neglecting the ascesis.[1] For learning from the bearer of your letter how you are managing with your ongoing illness, I found out that while you have had leisure to look at the entire divine Scripture, you have focused in on the most excellent book of the Psalms, and that you are eager to get at the meaning that is in each Psalm. And for this reason, above all else, I approve of what you're doing since I have fallen in love with this book as well, even as I have with all the Scripture. In fact, I once had a conversation with a certain learned old man who had devoted a great deal to the study of the Psalter. And so I also want to write to you to let you know how he explained it to me. For there was a certain grace and persuasiveness with his eloquent tale. This is what he said:

2. Everything that is in our Scripture, my child, is both old and new. It is God-breathed and profitable for teaching, as it is written.[2] But the book of Psalms has, in addition, a certain persuasive observation for those who

devote themselves to it. Now each book of Scripture serves its own purpose in what it relates, such as the Pentateuch telling of the birth of the world and the deeds of the patriarchs; of the exodus of Israel from Egypt, and the giving of the Law. The three volume work on Joshua, Judges and Ruth [the *Triteuch*] tells of the inheritance of the land and of the deeds of the judges and the genealogy of David. The Kings and Chronicles tell of the deeds of the kings, and Esdras tells of the release of the captives, the return of the people, and the building of the temple and the city. The prophets include prophecies concerning the advent of the Savior, calls for obedience concerning the commandments and for condemnation against their transgressors, as well as including prophecies for the gentiles. But the Book of Psalms is like a garden which besides bearing fruit in it that is found elsewhere—which it sets to music—brings to light its own special fruit which it accompanies in song along with the words.

3. It sings, for instance, of the Genesis events in Psalm 19: *The heavens declare the glory of God and the firmament proclaims the work of his hands*; and the 24th Psalm: *The earth is the Lord's and its fullness, its inhabitants and all who dwell in it; he laid its foundation upon the sea.* The accounts in Exodus, Numbers and Deuteronomy are sung beautifully in Psalm 78 and in the 114th [and 115th] Psalm: *In the exodus of Israel from Egypt, of the house of Jacob that came from a barbarous people, Judah became his sanctuary, Israel his dominion.* And again Psalm 105 says: *He sent his servant Moses, and Aaron whom he had chosen: he placed in them the words of his signs and of his wonders in the Land of Cham.*[3] *He sent darkness, and it darkened, and they rebelled against his words. He changed their waters into blood and killed their fish. Their land issued forth frogs in the palaces of their kings*, it says, *and the dog-fly and*

lice went into all their borders. And we find the whole entirety of this Psalm and Psalm 106 are written about these things. The matters concerning the priesthood and the tabernacle are referenced in Psalm 29,[4] which was sung when the tabernacle was brought out: *Bring to the Lord, sons of God, bring to the Lord the ram's offspring. Bring to the Lord glory and honor.*

4. The events of Joshua, son of Nun, and Judges are shown in Psalm 107: *And they built cities to inhabit, and sowed fields, and planted vineyards.* For under Joshua, son of Nun, the promised land was handed over to them. And when we read in this same Psalm frequently: *And they cried to the Lord in their afflictions, and from their distress he delivered them*, this indicates the events in the book of Judges. For when they cried out, he raised up judges at the time and saved the people from their afflictions. He sings the same things about the deeds of the kings in Psalm 20 saying: *Some trust in chariots and some in horses, but we will glory in the name of the Lord our God. They are brought down and fall. But we are raised up and restored. Lord, save the king and listen to us in whatever day we call upon you.* The events of Esdras are chanted in Psalm 126 of the Psalms of Ascent[5]: *When the Lord returned the captives of Zion we became as those who are comforted.* And again in Psalm 122: *I rejoiced when they said to me, "Let us go into the house of the Lord." Our feet stood in your courts, O Jerusalem. Jerusalem built as a city meant for joint possession. For that is where the tribes went up, the tribes of the Lord, as a testimony to Israel.*

5. The matters about which the Prophets speak are included in almost every one of the Psalms. In the 50th Psalm it talks about the Savior's time here on earth and that he would live here while being God: *The Lord will clearly come, our God, and he will not remain silent.* And in the 118th Psalm: *Blessed is the one who comes in the name of*

the Lord. We have blessed you from the house of the Lord. The Lord is God, and he has illumined us. And the 107th Psalm sings that this one [just mentioned] is the Word of the Father: *He sent his Word, and he healed them, and he delivered them from their ruin.* For the one who comes is God himself and the Word who is sent. And the voice of the Father sings in the 45th Psalm that this very Word is known to be the Son of God: *My heart has uttered a good Word.* And again in the 110th Psalm: *From the womb, before the morning star, I have begotten you.* For what else would you call someone born of the Father than his Word and Wisdom? This same book comprehends that it was known to whom the Father said, *Let there be light, and the firmament and all things,*[6] when it says, *By the Word of the Lord the heavens were established, and all their powers by the breath of his mouth.*[7]

6. Nor was it ignorant of Christ and his coming, but even makes a special mention of him in the 45th Psalm: *Your throne, O God is forever and ever. The scepter of your kingdom is a scepter of righteousness. You have loved righteousness and hated injustice. Because of this, God, your God has anointed you with the oil of gladness beyond your companions.* And just in case someone might think his coming was only in appearance,[8] it indicates that he would become man, and that this is the one through whom all things came to be, saying in the 87th Psalm: *The Mother of Zion will say, "A man, and a man is born in her, and the Most High himself established her. For this is the same as saying: And the Word was God. All things came into being through him.... And the Word became flesh.*[9] Because the Psalter knew all of this, as well as that he was from a virgin, it could not keep silent but immediately gives a clear indication of this in the 45th: *Listen, daughter, and see, and bend your ear, and forget your people and the house of your father, because the king has set his heart upon your*

beauty. This again is like what is said by Gabriel: *Greetings, favored one, the Lord is with you.*[10] For after proclaiming him the Christ, he immediately made known the human birth from the virgin, saying: *Listen, daughter*. Notice that Gabriel calls Mary by name since he has a different origin than she has. But David, from whose seed she happened to be, suitably addresses her as daughter.

7. After proclaiming that he would become man, it follows that the Psalter would make known his suffering in the flesh as well. Perceiving, then, there would be a treacherous scheme carried out by the Jews, it sings [about this] in the 2nd Psalm: *Why do the nations rage, and the peoples plot a vain thing? The kings of the earth rise up, and the rulers gather themselves together against the Lord and against his Christ.* In the 22nd Psalm it speaks from the Savior's own person of the kind of death he would undergo: *You have brought me down into the dust of death. For many dogs have surrounded me, the assembly of the evildoers has encompassed me. They pierced my hands and my feet. They counted out all my bones. And after they considered and beheld me, they divided my clothing among themselves and cast lots for my clothing.* To gouge the hands and the feet, what else can this indicate than that it is speaking about the cross? After teaching all these things it then adds that the Lord suffered these things not for himself, but for us. And he says this again in his own person in Psalm 88: *Your wrath has rested upon me*; and in Psalm 69: *Then I restored that which I did not take away.* For although he was not guilty, he died. But he suffered for us and endured the wrath that was meant for us because of our disobedience, as is spoken through the prophet Isaiah: *He took on our weaknesses.*[11] And this is mentioned for us in the 138th Psalm: *The Lord will pay them back for me*. And speaking also by the Spirit in Psalm 72: *And he will save*

the children of the poor, and he will humble the extortionists . . . for he has delivered the poor from the hand of the oppressor, and the laborer for whom no help was offered.

8. This is why it predicts his bodily ascension to the heavens and says in Psalm 24: *Lift up your gates, princes, and be lifted up you everlasting doors, and the king of glory will come in.* And in Psalm 47: *God ascends with a shout, the Lord with the voice of the trumpet.* It announces his being seated at the right hand and says in Psalm 110: *The Lord said to my Lord, "Sit at my right hand until I make your enemies a footstool for your feet."* And in the 9th Psalm it cries aloud about the destruction of the devil that occurred: *You sat upon the throne as one who judges righteousness; you censured the nations and the ungodly one perished.* For the fact that he has received judgment over all from the Father is not hidden [in the Psalms] either. Psalm 72 foretells that he would come as judge over all: *O God, give your judgment to the king and your righteousness to the son of the king to judge your people in righteousness and your poor with discernment.* And in the 50th Psalm it says: *He will summon the heaven above and the earth to sort out his people. And the heavens will announce his righteousness; for God is judge.* And in the 82nd Psalm we read: *God stands in the assembly of the gods, and in their midst he will judge the gods.* Even more, we learn from the Psalter about the calling of the nations in many places, but especially from Psalm 47: *Clap your hands all you nations, shout for joy to God with a voice of exultation.* And in the 72nd Psalm: *The Ethiopians will fall before him and his enemies will lick up the dust. The kings of Tarshish and the islands will offer gifts; the kings of Arabia and Saba will bring gifts. And all the kings of the earth will worship him, all the nations will serve him.* All these things are sung about in the Psalms, and in each of the other books of Scripture they are foretold as well.

9. Moreover, the old man said, I am not unaware that in every book of Scripture the same things concerning the Savior are given special prominence. In fact, this common argument is in all of them as all share in the same symphony of the Spirit. For just as one can find some things in the book of Psalms that are also in the others, so also material in the book of Psalms is often found in the others. Moses, for example, writes a song and Isaiah sings and Habakkuk prays with a song. And again, in each of the books you can perceive prophecies, legislation and historical accounts. For the same Spirit is over all, and each book ministers and fulfills the grace that is given to it according to the apportionment of the Spirit in each, whether it is prophecy, legislation, or a narration of the historical accounts, or the grace of the Psalms. And inasmuch as it is one and the same Spirit, certainly they are not all divided since the Spirit is indivisible by nature. Because the Spirit is given in its entirety, the manifestations and divisions of the Spirit are also distributed to each in order to serve the needs they are addressing. Furthermore, each [book] often ministers the Word as the Spirit instructs according to the need that has been laid bare. Therefore, as I said previously, when Moses enacts laws sometimes he prophesies, other times he sings. When the prophets prophesy sometimes they command: *Wash yourselves, be clean.*[12] *Cleanse your hearts from evil, Jerusalem;*[13] and other times they narrate history, such as Daniel does about Susannah,[14] and Isaiah about Rabshakeh and Sennacherib.[15] In the same way, the book of Psalms whose fundamental characteristic is that of song, sings within the full range of the voice accompanied by melodies about the matters recorded in detail in the other books, as I mentioned previously. But sometimes it also legislates: *Cease from evil and leave wrath behind.*[16] And: *Decline from evil and do*

good. Seek peace and pursue it.[17] And sometimes it also narrates about Israel's journey, or it prophecies about the Savior, just as was said previously.

10. Therefore let there be a common grace of the Spirit with all of Scripture and let the same grace which is in all of the books be found present in each book as the situation demands and as the Spirit wills. For the greater and the lesser in this do not differ according to need, since each unyieldingly fulfills and completes its own service. Indeed, the book of Psalms also has a certain grace of its own and an elevated style. For in addition to the other things it has in common with the other books, it has this amazing aspect—that within it the movements of each soul with all its changes and chastisements are detailed and worked out. The result is that anyone who really wants to receive or to understand from its limitless possibilities finds himself formed in just the way we find written there in the Psalms. For in the other books you only hear the law pronounced— what you need to do and not to do. And you listen and pay attention to the prophets as the only way to know the coming of the Savior, or you turn to the historical books in order to know about what the kings and the saints did. But when you listen to the book of the Psalms you not only learn about these things, but also apprehend and are taught the movements of your own souls. Consequently, when the passions take their toll on you, you are able to bring to bear the image of the words gleaned from the Psalms so they not only teach you, when you listen to them, to elude passions, but also what you need to say or do in order to heal the passions. Now there are words of warning also in the other books when they, for example, forbid evil. But in the Psalms you are also told how to keep away from evil. For instance, the command to repent is like this—repentance

means to stop sinning. But the book of Psalms also tells how to repent and what is necessary to say for repentance to actually take place. Moreover, Paul says: *Tribulation produces endurance for the soul, endurance produces character, and character hope, and this hope does not disappoint.*[18] In the Psalms too you are told how it is necessary to bear afflictions, and what you should say to someone who is suffering and what to say after the suffering has occurred. It relates how each person is tested and what words have been written and inscribed for those who hope in the Lord. In addition there is the command to give thanks in all things,[19] but the Psalms also teach what you should actually say when giving thanks. Then, hearing from another [book]: *As many as desire to pursue a godly life, they will be persecuted,*[20] from the Psalms we are also taught what to cry out when fleeing and what words should be offered to God while we are being persecuted, as well as what to say after the persecution when we have been delivered. We are encouraged to bless the Lord as well as to confess our praise to him. But in the Psalms we are even informed how one ought to praise the Lord and what words to say in order to confess him rightly. In fact, in every case we will find that these divine songs have been provided for us and the inner motions of our souls, and whatever condition we find ourselves in.

11. There is also this incredible thing in the Psalms. When people read what the saints say in the other books of Scripture or what is written about them, they don't see themselves in what is being spoken or written about. And when they hear what is being said they don't think it refers to themselves either, although they may go so far as to imitate the deeds they hear proclaimed and may even stand in awe of the zeal of these holy men: but no further. And when they take up the Psalter and en-

counter the prophecies about the Savior in certain Psalms, they treat them, too, with the same awe and reverence as they did when they encountered them in the other Scriptures. But the truly amazing thing is that when they come to the other Psalms they recognize them as being their very own words. And when they hear they are actually moved in their conscience. They feel as though they are the ones speaking and they take to heart the words of the songs as if they were their own. But for the sake of clarity, let us not hesitate to repeat what we've been saying, following the example of the blessed Apostle.[21] Many of the words of the patriarchs were spoken as their own. When Moses would speak, God would answer. And when both Elijah and Elisha called to the Lord while they were on Mount Carmel they would usually say: *As the Lord lives, before whom I stand this day.*[22] The principle words of the other holy prophets are words about the Savior, although most are directed toward the nations and Israel. Nevertheless no one would ever claim the words of the patriarchs as his own when he spoke, nor would anyone be bold enough to represent himself as speaking the words of Moses as if they were his own, nor would he have the effrontery to speak as his own the words of Abraham about the great Isaac or of Ishmael concerning the house-born slave— even if he felt there was some need or necessity that might compel him to do so. And if anyone would sympathize with someone who is suffering, and then at some point have a desire to say something more, he would never speak as Moses did: *Show yourself to me!*[23] Or again: *If you will forgive their sin, forgive. But if you will not forgive, then remove me from your book of life which you have written.*[24] Nor would anyone claim as his own the words of the prophets when they offered blame or praise, as though such a person could blame someone or offer praise like the prophets did. No one would represent himself as if he were speaking as his own the words: *As the Lord lives, before whom I stand this day.* For it surely is clear by now that anyone who encounters these books would not claim their words as his own, but would make clear that these are the words of the saints who are speaking. But with the Psalms, the amazing thing is that, apart from those that deal with the prophecies about the Savior and the nations, whenever anyone recites the rest of the Psalms he speaks the words as though they were his own and as though each of the Psalms was written specifically for him, and not as though someone else were speaking or as though they were meant for another. Instead he recites them as one who is speaking these things about himself as if he were accomplishing these very things himself. And in the very act of speaking them he is offering them to God on his own behalf. For he will not exhibit the same caution about these as he would with the words of the patriarchs, or Moses, or the other prophets. But above all, the one who sings them has the confidence that what he is speaking is as if it were his own and was written for him. For the Psalms address the deeds of those who keep the commandments as well as those who transgress them. And it is necessary that everyone be governed by these commandments, and whether they keep the commandment or transgress it, they should speak the words written that pertain to their particular situation.

12. It seems to me that these words often act like a mirror for the one who sings them. They allow him to see himself and the inner movements of his own soul in them. And when one recites them they produce that very effect. Indeed, for when someone hears what is read he receives the song as if it were speaking directly about him. He either repents, convicted by his conscience

which is sorely pricked, or after hearing about the hope in God and the help that awaits those who believe, he rejoices and begins to give thanks to God that such a gift is available to him. So then, when someone sings the 3rd Psalm, recognizing his own afflictions he will treat the words of the Psalm as his own as well. And when someone sings the 12th and the 17th Psalm, the boldness and prayer they proclaim speak to his own situation. And when one sings Psalm 51 he recites the words of repentance they contain as if they were his own. And when singing Psalms 54, 56, 57 and 142, he sings not as if another were being persecuted, but considers himself as the one who is suffering, and he sings to the Lord as if these words were his own. And finally, since each Psalm was dictated and composed by the Spirit, we find in them, as was said above, a better understanding of the inner movements of our own soul. All of what they say concerns us, and so their words come across as though they were our words. They serve as a reminder of the inner movements within us and as a corrective for our daily conduct.[25] For these are the things the singers are communicating and they can serve as examples and patterns for us.

13. Moreover, the same grace comes from the Savior, for he became man for us and offered his own body into death for us in order that everyone might be delivered from death. And wanting to bring to light his own citizenship that is heavenly and well pleasing, he typified it in himself so that some might no longer be so easily deceived by the enemy, having his victory over the devil which he accomplished for us as their security against stumbling. For this reason, he not only taught but also practiced what he taught, so that as each person hears what the Savior says, he might receive from him—just as if he were looking at an image in a mirror—the par-

adigm of what to do, hearing: *Learn from me, for I am meek and humble in heart.*[26] You could not find a more perfect example in virtuous teaching than what the Lord exemplified in himself. For whether in patient endurance, or love of humankind, or goodness, or manliness, or mercifulness, or righteousness—all of these you find occurring in him, with the result that there should be no aspect in virtue that is missing in anyone who comprehends this human life of his. For Paul knows this when he says: *Be imitators of me, just as I am of Christ.*[27] Those Greek legislators exhibited an extraordinary gift for speaking. But the Lord, who is truly Lord over all and concerned for those in distress, not only gave the law but also offered himself as a type, so that they might know the plans he is accomplishing by his power. It was surely because of this that, before the time he spent among us, he made this known in the Psalms in order that just as he made known in himself the earthly and the heavenly man by types, so also from the Psalms the one who is willing is able to learn the inner movements and dispositions of souls, finding in the Psalms both the healing and the correction needed for each movement.

14. If it is necessary to speak even more to the point, let us first of all admit that the entire divine Scripture teaches virtue and the truths of the faith, but that the book of Psalms contains the primary pattern for how souls are to be managed. For just as one who comes before a king carries with him a certain comportment and demeanor in what he says, so that he might not be thrown out as uneducated when he talks, in the same way for those striving toward virtue and wanting to comprehend the life of the Savior in the body, when they read this divine book it first of all brings to mind the inner movements of the soul and in this way further models and teaches petitioners such words as they

Letter to Marcellinus on the Psalms

should use. For it must first be observed that in this book there are Psalms that speak in narrative form, in exhortations, in prophecies, in the form of prayer, as well as in confession:

- There are those in narrative form, such as Psalms 19, 44, 49, 50, 73, 77, 78, 89, 90, 107, 114 [and 115], 127, 137;
- There are those in the form of prayer such as Psalms 17, 68, 90, 102, 132, 142;
- There are those that combine petition, prayer and entreaty, such as Psalms 5, 6, 7, 12, 13, 16, 25, 28, 31, 35, 38, 43, 54, 55, 56, 57, 59, 60, 61, 64, 83, 86, 88, 138, 140, 143;
- And having petition with thanksgiving, such as Psalm 139;
- And then there are those that are only in the form of petition, such as Psalms 3, 26, 69, 70, 71, 74, 79, 80, 109, 123, 130, 131;
- Those in the form of confession are Psalms 9 [and 10], 75, 92, 105, 106, 107, 108, 111, 118, 136, 138;
- Those having a combination of confession and narrative are Psalms 9 [and 10], 75, 106, 107, 118, 138;
- Psalm 111 has a combination of confession and narrative with adoration;
- And Psalm 37 is in the form of exhortation;
- Those that have prophecy are Psalms 21, 22, 45, 47, 76;
- And Psalm 110 has a reporting of events joined with prophecy;
- And exhortation as well as prescriptions are found in Psalms 29, 33, 81, 95, 96, 97, 98, 103, 104, 114;

- Exhortation with song is found in Psalm 150;
- And those describing the virtuous life are Psalms 105, 112, 119, 125, 133;
- Those proclaiming praise are Psalms 91, 113, 117, 135, 145, 146, 147, 148, 150;
- Those giving thanks are Psalms 8, 9 [and 10], 18, 34, 46, 63, 77, 85, 116,[28] 121, 122, 124, 126, 129, 144;
- Those proclaiming blessedness are Psalms 1, 32, 41, 119, 128;
- And Psalm 108 demonstrates how to sing with zeal;
- While Psalm 81 exhorts to fortitude;
- Psalms 2, 14, 36, 52, 53 accuse the ungodly and lawbreakers;
- While Psalm 4 is one of invocation;
- Those describing devotion are such as Psalms 20 and 64;
- Those boasting in the Lord proclaim words such as those found in Psalms 23, 27, 39, 40, 42, 62, 76, 84, 97, 99, 151 (LXX);
- Those that rebuke are Psalms 58 and 82;
- And those that contain the words of a hymn are Psalms 48 and 65;
- Psalm 66 is a Psalm of jubilation and about the resurrection;
- And another that contains only words of jubilation is Psalm 100.

15. Therefore, since the Psalms are arranged like this, it is possible for the readers to find in each, as was said above, the inner movements and conditions appropriate to the state of their own soul and identify the type of Psalm as well as the teaching contained in each. Some Psalms tell how a person is able to please the Lord and

make amends for his deeds and words, or how to give thanks to the Lord, or ensure that one does not fall into ungodliness for what he might say. For we will have to render an account to the Judge not only because of our works but also because of idle speech.[29] If therefore any of you should decide to bless someone, you have what you need to say, and how and in whom you are to say it in Psalms 1, 32, 41, 119 and 128. If you want to rebuke the plotting of the Jews against the Savior you have the 2nd Psalm. If you are suffering persecution from your own people, and you have many assembled against you, recite the 3rd Psalm. If in such affliction you called to the Lord and you want to give thanks that he heard you, sing Psalms 4, 75 and 116. And when you notice the wicked lying in wait wanting to do you harm and you want the Lord to listen to your prayer, rise up early in the morning and sing Psalm 5. And when you perceive threats from the Lord, if you see yourself disturbed because of these, you can recite Psalms 6 and 38. And if someone is plotting something against you, as Ahithophel did against David,[30] and you are informed about this, sing Psalm 7 and entrust yourself to God your deliverer.

16. And when you see the Savior's grace which has been spread abroad in every place as well as the salvation of the human race, if you want to address the Lord, sing Psalm 8. Moreover, if you want to celebrate the wine harvest by giving thanks to the Lord, you have again the same Psalm as well as Psalm 84.[31] For overcoming the enemy and the preservation of creation, not boasting in oneself but making known that the Son of God has accomplished this, recite the words of Psalm 9 [and 10] which is spoken to him. And whenever someone wants to stir up a lot of trouble for you, have your confidence in the Lord and sing Psalm 11. And when you witness the

arrogance of the crowd and increasing evil, so much so that nothing is considered holy among men, flee to the Lord and cry out Psalm 12. And if you are waylaid by the snare of your enemies, do not desert your post as if you were forgotten by God, but call upon the Lord, singing Psalm 13. And when you hear someone blaspheme against divine Providence, do not join with them in their ungodliness, but talk to God, reciting Psalms 14 and 53. And finally, if you want to learn what citizenship in the kingdom of heaven is like, sing Psalm 15.

17. If you are in need of prayer because of your adversaries and they are threatening your life, sings Psalms 17, 86, 88 and 141. And if you want to learn how Moses prayed, you have Psalm 90. And when you are saved from your enemies and delivered from your persecutors, you should sing Psalm 18. When you are amazed at the order of creation and the gift of divine Providence evident in it, as well as the sacred precepts of the Law, sing Psalms 19 and 24. When you see those who are afflicted, console them with prayer, speaking for them the words of Psalm 20. When you see yourself shepherded and cared for by the Lord, rejoice over this using Psalm 23. Your enemies surround you; nevertheless when you lift up your soul to God exclaim Psalm 25 and you will see *their iniquities come to no purpose.*[32] When your enemies persist, having nothing other than hands filled with blood and they are seeking to drag you down and destroy you, do not give their judgment over to man (for everything human is suspect); rather, considering God as a worthy judge—for He alone is just—speak Psalms 26, 35 and 43. And if they attack even more fiercely, with your enemies lining up in great numbers against you and looking down on you as if you have not yet been anointed,[33] and because of this they decide to make war, do not cower in fear, but sing Psalm 27. And if schemers

repeat their shameless behavior in order to deprive you of any rest from them, since the human nature is weak, cry out to God reciting the words in Psalm 28. And if when giving thanks you want to learn how one should make an offering to the Lord, chant Psalm 29 considering attentively what is being said. And finally, when you dedicate your home, i.e., the soul into which you welcome the Lord as well as the physical house in which you dwell bodily, give thanks and recite Psalms 30 and 127, which are among the Psalms of Ascent.

18. When you see yourself hated and persecuted by family and those you love because of the truth, you should not despair for yourself or them. And when you see those who are well known to you turning against you, don't be alarmed but instead separate yourself from them and, looking to the future, sing Psalm 31. Seeing those who are baptized and redeemed from their corrupt birth, and being amazed at the love of God for mankind, sing to them Psalm 32. And when you want to sing with the multitudes, gathering together people who live a righteous and upright life, sing Psalm 33. When you encounter your enemies and wisely escape and avoid their plots, if you want to give thanks, convene a group of men who are meek and sing Psalm 34 in their presence. And if you should see transgressors who have a party spirit set on evil, do not think they are evil *by nature*,[34] as the heretics say, but instead recite Psalm 36 and you will see that they themselves are the ones responsible for their sinning.[35] And if you see many lawless people doing evil and rising up against the weak, and you want to exhort someone not to turn towards them nor to emulate them, recite for yourself and the others Psalm 37.

19. Moreover if you see the enemy attacking when you set out to devote yourself to God (for this is the kind

of thing that riles him), and you want to shore yourself up against him, sing Psalm 39. And if when the enemy attacks you endure the afflictions and you want to learn the usefulness of endurance, sing Psalm 40. And when you see many who are poor and needy and you want to be merciful to them and urge others to do so as well by acknowledging those who have already been able to be merciful, recite Psalm 41 among them. Then, if while possessing a most excellent love for God you should hear of your enemies' reproach, do not be troubled; rather, noticing the imperishable fruit that comes from such love of God, comfort your own soul with hope in God. And being encouraged and calmed by the fact that this is your soul's plight in life, recite the 42nd Psalm. When you want to be reminded of the kindnesses of God which the fathers[36] experienced as well as about the exodus out of Egypt and the sojourn in the wilderness and how this demonstrates both the goodness of God and the ingratitude of men, you have Psalms 44, 78, 89, 105, 106, 107, 114 [and 115]. And when you flee to God for refuge and are delivered from the afflictions which befall you, if you want to give thanks to God and proclaim his love towards humanity which he has shown to you, you have Psalm 46.

20. But if you sin and, feeling ashamed, you repent and hope to be shown mercy, you have the words of confession and repentance that are found in Psalm 51. And if you are brought into discredit before an evil king, and you see the slanderer boasting, you have to step aside and speak to yourself what you have in Psalm 52. And when you are persecuted and slandered by someone who wants to betray you, as the Ziphites and other foreigners tried to do to David, do not be despondent; instead take courage in the Lord and praise him using the words in Psalms 54 and 56. And if you encounter a perse-

cutor and he unknowingly enters into the cave in which you also are hidden,[37] do not cower in fear since you have oracles that offer solace in such a situation as this, and these very words are inscribed in Psalms 57 and 142. And if someone plotting against you orders your house to be under surveillance, and you nevertheless escape, offer thanks to the Lord as though it were inscribed in stone on your soul, as a reminder that they did not utterly destroy you, and recite the words that are in Psalm 59. And if your enemies who oppress you insult you, and those who seem to be your friends discredit you by making a fool of you, and you get perplexed by their subtlety for a little while, nevertheless you should be comforted by singing to the Lord and reciting the words in Psalm 55. And against hypocrites and in the face of braggarts respond to their reproach with Psalm 58. And to those who rush savagely against you and want to take your life, oppose them by submitting yourself to God, and be of good courage. For as great as their rage is, when you submit to the Lord he is much greater, as it says in Psalm 62. And if when you are persecuted you are chased out into the wilderness, don't be afraid as if you were all alone. Instead, knowing you have God there, rise up early in the morning and sing to him Psalm 63. When you are being terrorized by your enemies and they do not stop laying traps for you—and they are searching for you everywhere—although they are many, by no means give in for their wounds are like those caused from the arrows of children.[38] In such a situation recite for yourself Psalms 64, 65, 70, and 71.

21. When you want to praise God with song, sing what is in Psalm 65. And if you want to teach someone about the resurrection, sing what is in Psalm 66. And while asking for mercy from God, praise him singing Psalm 67. And so that you may not be scandalized and

unsettled when you see the ungodly prospering in peace while the righteous are living with tribulations, recite for yourself what is in Psalm 73. And when God is angry at his people, you possess prudent words of comfort about this in Psalm 74. And when it is necessary for you to offer confession, sing Psalms 9 [and 10], 75, 92, 105, 106, 107, 108, 111, 118, 136 and 138. When you desire to put to shame the opinions of the Greeks and the heretics because knowledge of God does not come from them but is found only in the catholic church, knowing this is the case you are able to sing and to recite the words in Psalm 76. And when enemies occupy in advance the escape routes and you are in great distress, although this troubles you, do not despair—pray instead. And if you are heard when you cry out to God, give thanks to him saying the words in Psalm 77. And if your enemies persist in their attacks as they profane the house of God, kill the saints, and throw their bodies to the vultures, don't be intimidated by their savagery, cowering in fear; instead suffer along with those who are suffering and make an entreaty to God reciting the 79th Psalm.

22. And on the feast day, when you want to sing to the Lord, call together the servants of God and sing in their midst Psalms 81 and 95. And again, when all of your enemies gather together from every quarter and make threats against the house of God while they make treaties against godliness—so that you do not become disheartened because of their numbers and their power —you have as an anchor the hope that is in the words of the 83rd Psalm. And when you see the house of God and his eternal tabernacles and you find yourself longing for them as the Apostle did,[39] say for yourself Psalm 84. And when wrath subsides[40] and captivity is taken captive, if you want to give thanks you have the words of Psalms 85 and 126 to speak. And if you want to know the difference

between the catholic church and the schismatics and to confound the schismatics, you are able to speak what is written in Psalm 86.[41] And if you want to encourage yourself and others towards godliness—and since hope in God will never be put to shame but rather equips the soul so that it is not afraid—praise God reciting Psalm 91. Do you want to sing on the Sabbath? You have Psalm 92.

23. Do you want to give thanks on the Lord's Day? You have Psalm 24. Do you want to sing praises on the second day of the week? Recite the words in Psalm 48. Do you want to offer glory to God on the Day of Preparation?[42] You have the song of praise in Psalm 93, for on that day the crucifixion occurred and the house of God was fortified to further hinder the attack of the enemies. And because of this victory it is fitting to sing to God the words found in Psalm 93. And if you are held captive and the house [of God] is destroyed and then is built up again, sing the words in Psalm 96. When your land receives a reprieve from wars and is finally at rest and governed by the Lord, if you want to sing about this, you have the 97th Psalm. Do you want to sing praises on the fourth day of the week? You have the words of Psalm 94.[43] For it was then, when he was about to be betrayed, that the Lord began to exact vengeance against the judgment of death and boldly to triumph over it. When therefore you are reading the Gospel you should know that the fourth day of the week indicates when the Jews took counsel against the Lord. Seeing him, then, emboldened against the devil with vengeance on your behalf, sing the words which are in Psalm 94. Furthermore, when you see the providence of the Lord and his dominion over all things, and want to teach some people about faith and obedience, persuade them first to confess him in praise, singing Psalm 100. And when learning of his power for judging, but also that when the Lord

judges he mixes mercy with judgment, if you want to approach him you have for this the words which are in Psalm 101.

24. Because our nature is weak, if the anxieties of life overwhelm you and you become like a beggar and want to be consoled, you have the 102nd Psalm. And since it is fitting for us to give thanks to God for all things and in all situations, when you want to praise him, you have the words of Psalms 103 and 104 to stir up your soul. Do you want to praise God, and to know how and before whom you should sing praises as well as what is appropriate to say when you praise him? You have Psalms 105, 107, 135, 146, 147, 148 and 150. Do you have faith, as the Lord said, and when you are praying do you believe what you are saying? Then recite Psalm 116. Do you consider yourself as one ascending towards God with your deeds, so much so that you say: *I forget what lies behind, while I strain for what is ahead*?[44] For each step along your journey you have the 15 Psalms of Ascent to recite.[45]

25. You were taken captive by alien thoughts and you sensed their seduction, but after realizing what they were doing you stopped doing anything further. But while you endured them you found yourself falling into sin. Fall on your knees then and lament over your condition, as the people of old did, reciting the words of Psalm 137. When experiencing trials that test you, if you want to give thanks after successfully enduring the trials, you have Psalm 139. Are you troubled again by your enemies and want to be delivered? Recite the words in Psalm 140. Do you want to offer supplication? Do you want to pray? Sing Psalms 5 and 143. If an enemy tyrant rises against you and the people, such as Goliath did against David, do not cower in fear. Instead, believe as David did and recite what is in Psalm 144. Then, being amazed at everything God has done and remembering the good deeds

he has done for you and everyone else, if you want to praise God, speak the words of David as he spoke them in the 145th Psalm. Do you want to sing to the Lord? You are given the words to utter in Psalms 93 and 98. If, though insignificant, you are chosen as some kind of ruler over your brothers,[46] do not rise up in opposition against them. Instead, giving glory to the Lord who chose you, sing for yourself Psalm 151 which belongs to David. And if you want to sing praises, pay attention to those Psalms having Alleluias, such as Psalms 105, 106, 107, [111], 112, 113, 114 [and 115], 116, 117, 118, 119, 135, 136, 146, 147, 148, 149, and 150.[47]

26. When you want to sing about the Savior on your own in private, you will find such things about the Savior more or less in every Psalm, but you especially have Psalms 45 and 110 which speak of his genuine generation from the Father and the advent of his incarnation. And Psalms 22 and 69 foretell the divine cross and how great the treachery was that he endured for us and how much he suffered. And Psalms 2 and 109 indicate both the treachery and the baseness of the Jews as well as the betrayal by Judas Iscariot. And Psalms 21, 50 and 72 indicate his kingdom and his power for judging as well as the advent of his incarnation for us and the calling of the gentiles. And Psalm 16 brings to light his resurrection from the dead, while Psalms 24 and 47 announce his ascension to the heavens. When you read Psalms 93, 96, 98 and 99, you should be capable of contemplating the blessings which have come to us from the Savior through his suffering.

27. Such then is the kind of help for humanity that can be gleaned from the book of Psalms. It contains Psalms that are unique to its genre as well as others that foretell the advent of our Lord and Savior Jesus Christ in the body often found in the prophets, as was said above.

But we cannot pass over the question of why its words are put to melody and song. For some of the more simple-minded among us, although they believe the words are God-breathed, nevertheless think that that the reason for rendering the Psalms in melody is primarily for the delight of the ear. But this is not the case. For Scripture does not necessarily seek out what is pleasing and persuasive, and the Psalms in turn are constituted primarily for the benefit of the soul—and for any number of other reasons, but mainly these two: First, because it was fitting for the divine Scripture to offer praise to God not just by following a mere sequential narrative, but to do so in a voice that is wide ranging. Sometimes Scripture just relates the simple sequence of events such as what is recorded in the Law and the Prophets and all the historical accounts as well as the New Testament. But other times it speaks more freely, such as what we find in the phrases of the Psalms and odes and songs that are in it. For these remind humanity to love God with all our strength and power. Secondly, just as the harmony of instruments playing together produces one symphony, in the same way then the Psalms disclose the full range of the inner movements in the soul. For in the soul these movements range from reason to desire to anger, and from these inner movements come the outer actions of the bodily members. The mind, however, does not intend for man to be discordant or at variance with himself. And so, the best people operate on the basis of reason; base people, however, act when they are provoked, as for instance Pilate does when he says: *I find nothing worthy of death in him*,[48] and yet concurs with the verdict of the Jews. Some people desire base things but are not able to do them, such as the elders against Susannah; others may not commit adultery but they steal, or they don't steal but they commit murder; or they don't murder but they blaspheme.

28. In order that there be no such disturbance in us, reason would have the soul possess the mind of Christ, as the Apostle said,[49] furnishing this mind of Christ as a guide. Human beings constantly struggle to conquer what is ruling over the members of the body to bring those members into obedience to reason. For just as the plectrum plucks the strings in harmony, so might the man who engages the Psalter—and by the Spirit devotes himself entirely to it—bring all the members of his body and his emotions into submission. In this way he can serve the will of God. The harmonious reading of the Psalms provides just such an image and example of calm reasoning and settled condition. For just as the thoughts of the soul are made known and declared through the words that bear them, so also the spiritual harmony in the soul—which the Lord desires to be symbolized by the words accompanied with melody—is exemplified by the harmonious odes that are sung, and the Psalms that are recited with music. The desire of the soul is that it be ordered well, as it is written: *Is anyone among you happy? Let him sing.*[50] And so whatever is troubled, rough or disorderly in the soul is smoothed out. The distressed are truly healed when we sing: *Why are you perplexed, O my soul, and why do you disturb me?*[51] And our helplessness is acknowledged when we sing: *But my feet were shaken a little.*[52] And those who fear are strengthened in hope when they sing: *The Lord is my helper, and I will not be afraid. What can man do to me?*[53]

29. Therefore those who do not recite the divine songs in this way are not singing wisely. They may be enjoying themselves but there is cause for blame because: *A hymn of praise is not suitable in the mouth of a sinner.*[54] But when they sing in the way mentioned earlier—so

that the melody for the words is produced from the rhythm of the soul and in harmony with the spirit—these kinds of people sing not only with the tongue but also with the mind, and thus are extremely helpful not only for themselves but also for those who want to listen. Therefore when the blessed David sang in this way for Saul, he not only pleased God but also drove away the madness and confusion of Saul and calmed his soul.[55] Similarly when the priests sang like this they calmed the souls of the people by uniting them with the heavenly chorus which they summoned. To sing the Psalms with melodies then is not so much because one is eager for a pleasing sound but is rather a sure sign of the harmony of the mind with the soul. And a harmonious reading such as this is an indication of a well-trained and tranquil state of mind. In fact to praise God with the pleasing sound of cymbals, and with the harp and the ten-stringed psalter[56] was again a symbol and sign of how the members of the body work together just as the strings of an instrument are properly regulated. Or, the cymbals are symbolic of the thoughts of the soul by which, finally, all these members of the body are set in motion and live through the sound and the sanction of the Spirit. Thus, we have what is written: *By the Spirit was man made alive and the deeds of the body are put to death.*[57] For in the same way, when one sings well he becomes in tune with his soul just as one is led from being out of balance to being in balance. The result is that when one is well grounded in his nature he will not be distraught over something but instead takes a more positive attitude towards it and inevitably receives more of what he desires in the future. For when the melody is joined to the words you forget what you are suffering and find yourself rejoicing instead, seeing things with the mind of Christ and dwelling on what is best.

30. Therefore it is necessary, O child, for each person who is reading this book to know that everything in it is God-breathed. He should take whatever help he can from it as though he were picking from the fruits of paradise, having them within the range of his sight when the need arises. For the words of this book can serve as a guide for every aspect of human life, embracing both the disposition of the soul as well as gauging the movements of the thoughts. And nothing more than these can be found in human beings. For whether there is a need for repentance or confession, or tribulation and trials overtake you, or you are persecuted, or delivered from those who were plotting against you, or if you are deeply grieved and troubled and suffer in some way, as was noted above, or you see yourself prospering while your enemy is hindered, or you want to sing or to give thanks or to bless the Lord—you can find instructions in the divine Psalms. So take what the Psalms say about each of these things and speak them as though they were written for you, and as what is written affects you, offer those words to the Lord.

31. Let no one, indeed, attempt to embellish this Psalter with extraneous persuasive words, or attempt to change or alter in any way what is said there. Instead let him speak or chant in simplicity what is written, saying it just as it is, so that when the men who supplied these [words] join with us in prayer[58] they might recognize these words as their own. But even more so, when the Spirit, who speaks in the saints, sees the words from him resonating in them, he might come to our aid. For just as the life of the saints is so much better than any other, so also someone might rightly say that their words are composed much better and stronger than ours are. For in these things they were pleasing to God, and when they spoke, as the Apostle has said: *They conquered kings, ad-*

ministered justice, obtained promises, stopped the mouth of the lions, quenched the powerful fire, fled the mouth of the sword, made strength from weakness, grew mighty in war, turned the tide against the foreign encampment, and women received their dead by resurrection.[59]

32. So then, let each person who recites these Psalms now take heart because God will readily hear those who petition him through them. For if someone speaks the Psalms while he is suffering affliction, he will gain great comfort from them. And if he experiences testing and persecution while singing in this way, he will be revealed to be more worthy and will be protected by the Lord who watched over the one who first spoke these words. The devil will flee from people like this and his demons will be routed. If someone has sinned, when he recites these Psalms he will feel ashamed of himself and stop sinning. If he hasn't sinned, he will find himself rejoicing because he is straining forward towards *what lies ahead.*[60] And while he is contending for the prize he is strengthened as he sings in this way. He will never be moved from the truth, but he will put to shame the deceivers and the ones who prey upon those who go astray. But man is not the guarantor of this; rather, the divine Scripture itself is. For God commanded Moses to write the great song,[61] and to teach the people. He was appointed as their ruler and he was the one ordered to write Deuteronomy and to have it on hand and always to attend to the words contained in it[62] as the words in it are sufficient both for calling virtue to mind as well as bringing assistance to those who study them with knowledge. For instance, at the time that Joshua, son of Nun, entered the land, when he saw the enemies in their battle array and the kings of the Amorites all assembled for war, he read this prayer about arms and swords in Deuteronomy in the hearing of all, reminding them of

the words of the law[63] and equipping the people with them so they would prevail over their enemies. And when King Josiah discovered the book and read it in the hearing of all,[64] he no longer feared their enemies. And whenever war against the people was at hand, they had the ark with the tablets of the law go before everyone and it defended them as an auxiliary force against all those assembled for battle against them, unless there was some sin or hypocrisy that took hold among the ones carrying the ark or among the people. For there is need of faith and a noble disposition in order that the law might support those things offered in prayer.

33. Indeed, the old man said, I also have heard from wise men that in ancient Israel, by merely reading the Scriptures, demons were put to flight and the schemes they hatched against men were utterly brought to ruin. This is why, he said, all those are worthy of condemnation who abandon the Scriptures. They conclude that words foreign to Scripture are more persuasive and style themselves exorcists when they use them. But they are just playing around and make themselves a laughing-stock when they do things like this. The Jewish sons of Sceva[65] who were ill-treated by the demons were like this when they attempted to exorcise the demons by this method. For when the demons heard these things from them they made sport of them. But the demons were afraid of the words of the saints—they couldn't bear to hear them. For the Lord is in the words of the Scriptures which the demons cannot bear. And so they cry out: *I beg of you, do not torment me before the time.*[66] For they were scorched after merely encountering the Lord's presence. Paul also commands the unclean spirit in this way,[67] and the demons submit to the disciples as well.[68] And the hand of the Lord came upon Elisha the prophet and he prophesied about the waters to the three kings

when the musician played according to his command.[69] Even now, if someone is troubled by trials, let him utter these Psalms and he will not only help the sufferer but also declare his own faith true and certain. The result is that when he prays in this way to God, God will grant perfect healing to those in need. Knowing this, the saint says in Psalm 119: *I will meditate on your righteous deeds. I will not forget your words.*[70] And again: *Your righteous acts were songs to me in my dwelling place.*[71] For with these Psalms they also gained deliverance, saying: *Were it not that your law is my meditation, then I would have been destroyed in my humiliation.*[72] This is also why Paul fortified his own disciples, saying: *Practice these things; stand firm in them in order that your progress may be made known.*[73] So you too should practice wisely reading these Psalms in this way, so that you might comprehend what is meant in each, being led by the Spirit. And in this way you also will be able to emulate the kind of life which those God-bearing holy men who spoke these Psalms had.

NOTES

1. Introduction to Athanasius' Letter to Marcellinus

1. Craig Blaising, *Ancient Christian Commentary on Scripture: Psalms 1-50*, vol. VII (Downers Grove, IL: InterVarsity Press, 2008), xx.
2. See the note on the *Defense Against the Arians*, found in NPNF 2 4:148.
3. Rom 8:26.
4. *Letter to Marcellinus* 10.
5. *Letter to Marcellinus* 12.
6. *Letter to Marcellinus* 10.
7. *Letter to Marcellinus* 11.
8. Ibid.
9. *Letter to Marcellinus* 27.
10. Ibid.
11. *Letter to Marcellinus* 1.
12. *Letter to Marcellinus* 14.
13. *Letter to Marcellinus* 15.
14. *Letter to Marcellinus* 30.
15. *Letter to Marcellinus* 33.

2. Athanasius: Letter to Marcellinus

1. Spiritual discipline which early Christians practiced. The Greek word is based on the idea of athletic training which Christians appropriated for disciplining both the body and the soul.
2. 2 Tim 3:16.
3. I.e., Ham.
4. The heading of Psalm 28 in the Septuagint is "A Psalm of David when the Tabernacle went forth."
5. Psalms 120-134 [119-133 in the Septuagint] are a group of 15 Psalms known as the Psalms of Ascent, or the Gradual Psalms.
6. Gen 1:3ff.
7. Ps 33:6.
8. Athanasius speaks here against the ancient heresies of Docetism and Gnosticism.
9. Jn 1:1-2, 14.
10. Lk 1:28.
11. Isa 53:4.
12. Isa 1:16.

13. Jer 4:14.
14. Dan 12.
15. Isa 36-37.
16. Ps 37:8 [36:8 LXX].
17. Ps 34:14 [33:15 LXX].
18. Rom 5:3-5.
19. 1 Thess 5:18.
20. 2 Tim 3:12.
21. In his epistles, Paul at times will repeat words or phrases for clarity, such as he does in Gal. 1:9, Phil 4:4, etc.
22. Cf. 1 Kgs 17:1; 2 Kgs 3:14.
23. Ex 33:13.
24. Ex 32:32.
25. The Greek word has the idea of citizenship attached to it.
26. Mt 11:29.
27. 1 Cor 11:1.
28. The Hebrew and English Bibles combine Psalms 114 and 115 from the Septuagint.
29. Mt 12:36.
30. Cf. 2 Sam 15:31ff.
31. The heading of Psalms 8 and 83 in the LXX (Psalms 8 and 84 in the Hebrew and English] is "To the end for the wine-presses, a Psalm for the sons of Korah." Although the two Psalms themselves seem to have little to say about the wine presses, it would seem that these were perhaps still Psalms sung at the wine harvest.
32. Athanasius' text differs slightly from both the Hebrew [of Psalm 25:8] and the LXX of Psalm 24:8, which speaks of instructing sinners in the way.
33. Here one would assume that Athanasius is speaking about the anointing with oil that accompanied the rite of Baptism which would establish one as a child of God.
34. Emphasis translator's.
35. Athanasius seems to be battling the long held view of determinism and fatalism among heretical factions, such as the Gnostics and others, that there are some human beings whose very nature is predestined for evil and who thus have no opportunity to be redeemed.
36. The patriarchs.
37. Cf. 1 Sam 23:19-24.
38. LXX Ps 64:7.
39. Perhaps a reference to Hebrews 8 and 9.
40. Psalms 85 and 126 would indicate Athanasius here means the wrath of God.
41. The Greek text had Ps 86 in the LXX listed here, but the context would seem to indicate Athanasius has in mind Ps 87 (LXX), which would be Psalm 86 in the Hebrew and English.
42. Lit." Parasceve" = the day of preparation before the Jewish Sabbath.
43. In the LXX, the heading of the Psalm reads "A Psalm of David on the fourth day of the week," lit. "the fourth of the Sabbath."

Notes

44. Phil 3:13.
45. The 15 Psalms of Ascent are Psalms 120-134 (or Psalms 119-133 LXX) each of which has an ascription that reads "Song of the Ascents." They are also known as the Gradual Psalms. Scholars are not agreed as to the exact occasion for which they were used. They were perhaps sung by worshipers as they ascended the road to Jerusalem to celebrate the three festivals of unleavened bread, weeks, and tabernacles (booths) prescribed for all males in Deut 16:16. Or perhaps they were sung by the Levites when they ascended the temple steps, which were fifteen in number. There are other possibilities as well.
46. Such as Joseph was, as recorded in Gen 41ff.
47. Here as elsewhere we have provided the Psalms according to their English/Hebrew numbering. Many English Bibles, however, translate the Alleluia's as "Praise the Lord," and so often don't include the actual word. In the Septuagint Psalms Athanasius lists, as well as in many of their counterparts in Hebrew, the word "alleluia" is found in the beginning of the Psalms as a heading. And so that is why they are referred to as the "Alleluia Psalms." For reference, the corresponding Septuagint Psalms Athanasius lists in the original Greek are: 104, 105, 106, 111, 112, 113, 114, 115, 116, 117, 118, 134, 135, 145, 146, 147, 148, 149, and 150. He left out Psalm 110 [111 in English], which is also an Alleluia Psalm in the Septuagint, and so we have included it in the list, although in brackets. Also, Psalm 147 in English combines two alleluia Psalms, Psalms 146 and 147, from the LXX.
48. Jn 18:38.
49. 1 Cor 2:16.
50. Cf. James 5:13.
51. Ps 42:5,11; 43:5 [41:6, 12; 42:5 LXX].
52. Ps 73:2 [72:2 LXX].
53. Ps 118:6 [117:6 LXX].
54. Sir 15:9.
55. 1 Sam 16:23.
56. Ps 150:3-5.
57. Rom 8:13.
58. Perhaps referring here to the fact that the early church believed that the saints who wrote these words in the Old Testament, along with the whole company of heaven, joined them in the liturgy.
59. Heb 11:33-35.
60. Phil 3:16.
61. Deut 31:19.
62. Deut 17:18-19.
63. Josh 8:34-35.
64. 2 Kgs 22:8-11.
65. Acts 19:14-16.
66. Cf. Lk 8:28.
67. Acts 16:18.
68. Lk 10:17.
69. 2 Kgs 3:15.

70. Ps 118:16 [LXX]; cf. Ps 119:16.
71. Ps 118:54 [LXX]; cf. Ps 119:54.
72. Ps 118:92 [LXX]; cf. Ps 119:92.
73. 1 Tim 4:15.

ABOUT THE AUTHOR

Joel Elowsky, (Ph.D. Drew University) is a professor of Historical Theology and coordinator of the International Seminary Exchange Programs at Concordia Seminary, St. Louis. He is the director of the Seminary's Center for the Study of Early Christian Texts. He is the author/editor of over a half dozen books, including a two-volume *Commentary on the Gospel of John* (ACCS), a volume on the Holy Spirit entitled *We Believe in the Holy Spirit* as part of the Ancient Christian Doctrine series, a new English translation of the *Encyclopedia of the Early Church*, edited by Angelo Di Berardino, published by InterVarsity Press. He has also contributed chapters to other books as well as numerous articles and reviews.

www.ingramcontent.com/pod-product-compliance
Lightning Source LLC
Chambersburg PA
CBHW052127070526
44586CB00016B/2120